MATH ON

MARS

By Mark A. Harasymiw

Gareth Stevens
PUBLISHING

Please visit our website, www.garethstevens.com. For a free color catalog of all our high-quality books, call toll free 1-800-542-2595 or fax 1-877-542-2596.

Cataloging-in-Publication Data

Names: Harasymiw, Mark.
Title: Math on Mars / Mark A. Harasymiw.
Description: New York : Gareth Stevens Publishing, 2016. | Series: Solve it! math in space | Includes index.
Identifiers: ISBN 9781482449396 (pbk.) | ISBN 9781482449334 (library bound) | ISBN 9781482449235 (6 pack)
Subjects: LCSH: Mathematics–Problems, exercises, etc.–Juvenile literature. | Mars (Planet)–Juvenile literature.
Classification: LCC QA39.3 H35 2016 | DDC 510.76–dc23

First Edition

Published in 2017 by
Gareth Stevens Publishing
111 East 14th Street, Suite 349
New York, NY 10003

Designer: Laura Bowen
Editor: Therese Shea

Photo credits: Cover, p. 1 (Mars) Twin Design/Shutterstock.com; cover, p. 1 (metal banner) Eky Studio/Shutterstock.com; cover, pp. 1–24 (striped banner) M. Stasy/Shutterstock.com; cover, pp. 1–24 (stars) angelinast/Shutterstock.com; cover, pp. 1–24 (math pattern) Marina Sun/Shutterstock.com; pp. 4–24 (text box) Paper Street Design/Shutterstock.com; p. 5 (main) Huntster/Wikimedia Commons; p. 5 (inset) MarcelClemens/Shutterstock.com; p. 7 Macrovector/Shutterstock.com; pp. 9, 11, 13, 15, 17, 19, 21 courtesy of NASA.com.

Printed in the United States of America

CPSIA compliance information: Batch #CS16GS: For further information contact Gareth Stevens, New York, New York at 1-800-542-2595.

CONTENTS

Words in the glossary appear in **bold** type the first time they are used in the text.

MISSION TO MARS

Sometimes we can see Mars in the night sky. It looks like a red star, but it's really a planet. Its color tells us there's a lot of iron on the surface. When iron mixes with the gas oxygen, it creates iron oxide—rust!

There's so much more to learn about this world. That's why unmanned spacecraft have been sent to visit it. They're collecting and sending back **data** every day. However, in this book, you're going to the "Red Planet" to seek out facts for yourself. Let's get ready for lift-off!

YOUR MISSION

Just as scientists solve different kinds of problems, you need to use different math operations and measurements to learn about Mars. Look for the upside-down answers to check your work.

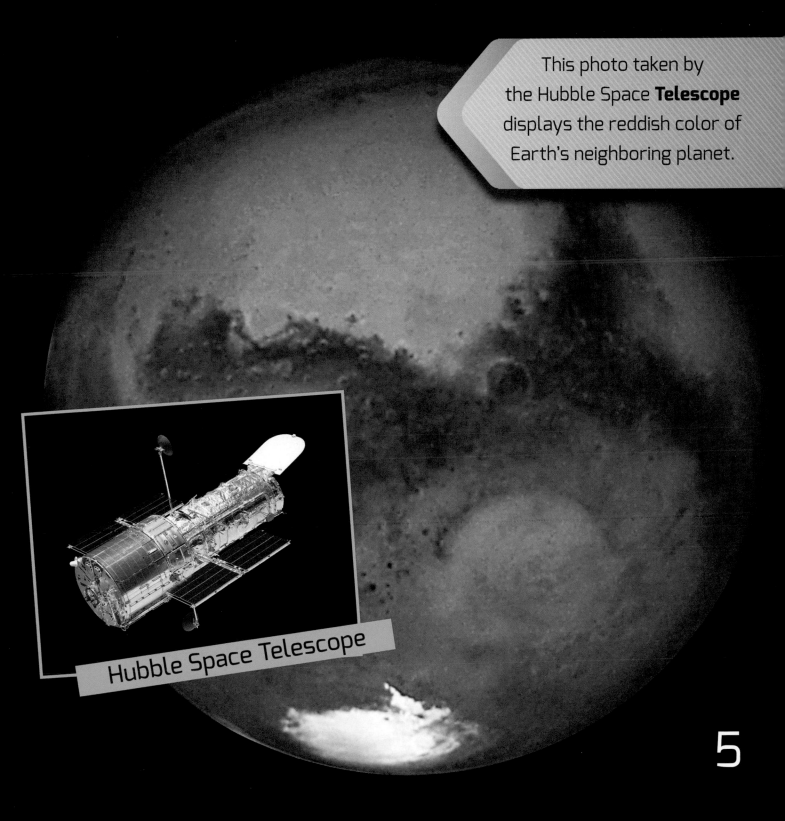

This photo taken by the Hubble Space **Telescope** displays the reddish color of Earth's neighboring planet.

Hubble Space Telescope

5

WHERE IS IT?

Mars is the fourth planet from the sun, between Earth and Jupiter. It's also the outermost terrestrial planet. "Terrestrial" means it's a **dense**, rocky world with a solid surface, unlike the planets made of gases. Mars is the second-smallest planet in our **solar system**, after Mercury.

YOUR MISSION

The imaginary line that runs from one side of a planet through its center to the other side is the diameter. The diameter of Earth is 7,926 miles. The diameter of Mars is 3,706 fewer miles than Earth's diameter. Find the diameter of Mars.

$$7{,}926 - 3{,}706 = \,?$$

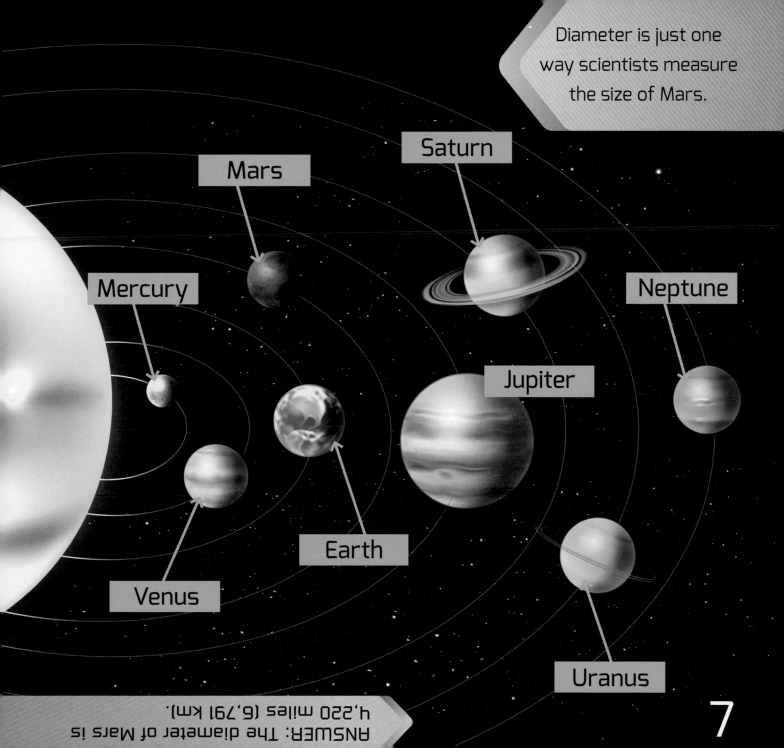

Diameter is just one way scientists measure the size of Mars.

Saturn

Mars

Mercury

Neptune

Jupiter

Earth

Venus

Uranus

ANSWER: The diameter of Mars is 4,220 miles (6,791 km).

MOONS OF MARS

The planet Mars gets its name from the war god in ancient Roman stories. The war god had horses called Phobos and Deimos in Greek stories. These names were given to Mars's two moons. Phobos has lines on its surface that make scientists at NASA (National Aeronautics and Space Administration) think it will break into pieces someday!

YOUR MISSION

Phobos is larger than Deimos. The area of Phobos is 1,548 square kilometers, and the area of Deimos is 483 square kilometers. What's the difference between the areas of Phobos and Deimos?

1,548 – 483 = ?

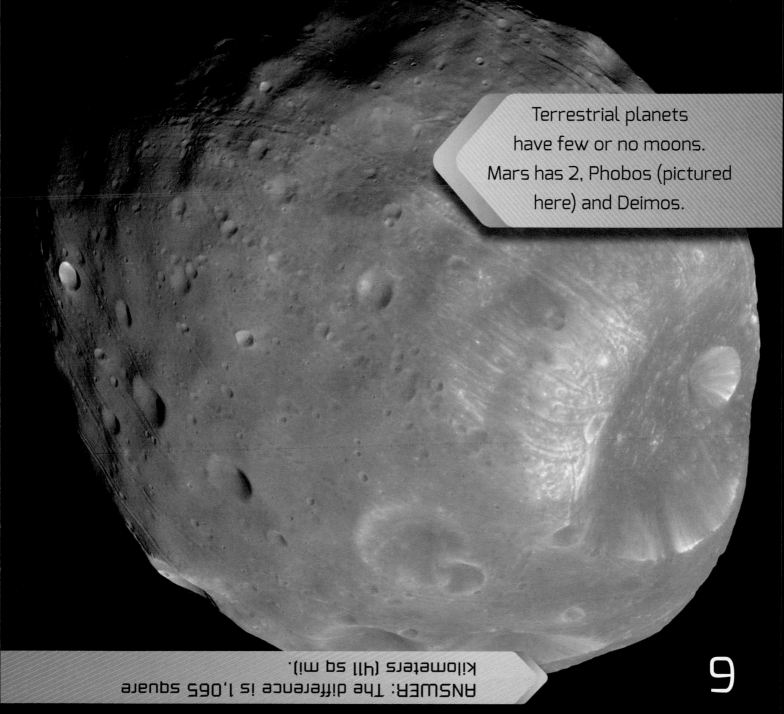

Terrestrial planets
have few or no moons.
Mars has 2, Phobos (pictured
here) and Deimos.

ANSWER: The difference is 1,065 square
kilometers (411 sq mi).

LIKE EARTH

Mars is similar to Earth in some ways. It has weather such as clouds and winds. It's **tilted** like Earth is, which means it has seasons. Its day is a similar length to Earth's, too. Scientists think Mars was even more like Earth billions of years ago. It was probably warmer than it is now. It likely also had rivers, lakes, and oceans.

YOUR MISSION

The amount of time it takes a planet to rotate, or spin around, completely is called its day. Earth's day is 23 hours 56 minutes long. Mars completes a rotation once every 24 hours 37 minutes. How much longer is Mars's day?

24 hours 37 minutes – 23 hours 56 minutes = ?

Mars has Earthlike land features, such as **volcanoes**, plains, and valleys.

ANSWER: Mars's day is 41 minutes longer than Earth's.

OLYMPUS MONS

Mars is home to the tallest volcano in the solar system, Olympus Mons. It's 16 miles (26 km) high! The largest volcano on Earth is Mauna Loa in Hawaii. It's about 10.6 miles (17 km) high. Scientists think Olympus Mons is so large because Mars's **crust** doesn't move as Earth's does. **Lava** keeps piling up, making the volcano grow.

YOUR MISSION

Earth **orbits** the sun more quickly than Mars does. It takes about 365 days for Earth to journey around the sun. That's 1 Earth year. A year on Mars is about 322 Earth days longer than this. Find out how many Earth days a year on Mars is.

$$365 + 322 = ?$$

Olympus Mons is 374 miles (602 km) in diameter. This picture shows that Olympus Mons is just about the same size as the US state of Arizona!

approximate size
of Arizona

ANSWER: Mars's year is about 687 Earth days.

WEAR SOMETHING WARM!

The average temperature on Mars is –81°F (–63°C). One reason Mars is so much colder than Earth is that Mars is farther from the sun. Like the other planets, Mars has an elliptical, or egg-shaped, orbit around the sun. That means sometimes it's closer to the sun than at other times.

YOUR MISSION

Mars's average distance from the sun is about 142 million miles, while Earth's average distance from the sun is about 93 million miles. How much farther from the sun is Mars compared to Earth on average?

142 million – 93 million = ?

Mars is so cold that even some gases, such as carbon dioxide, freeze! The ice on Mars is made up of both frozen water and frozen carbon dioxide.

ANSWER: Mars is about 49 million miles (79 million km) farther from the sun on average.

15

MUCH LESS MASS

Besides being much, much colder than Earth, Mars's **gravity** is also much weaker than Earth's. The amount of gravity a planet has depends on its **mass**. Mars has less mass than Earth. In fact, it only has about 10 percent the mass of Earth! So, Mars has less gravity than Earth. That means objects would weigh less on Mars than on Earth.

YOUR MISSION

You'd weigh less on Mars, too! A person who weighs 50 pounds on Earth would weigh about 19 pounds on Mars. If a person weighed twice that amount on Earth, how much would they weigh on Earth and Mars?

$50 \times 2 = ?$ $19 \times 2 = ?$

If Mars and Earth could be photographed side by side, it would look something like this.

ANSWER: The person would weigh 100 pounds (45 kg) on Earth and 38 pounds (17 kg) on Mars.

VISITORS TO MARS

Mariner 4 was the first spacecraft to successfully travel to Mars, flying past it in 1965. It took photographs of the planet. These were the first photos taken of a planet other than Earth! It operated for 3 more years, studying the sun, after this NASA **mission**. The spacecrafts *Viking 1* and *Viking 2* actually landed on Mars in 1976.

YOUR MISSION

The United States launched, or sent into space, a number of missions to Mars in the 1960s. According to the chart on page 19, what fraction of the missions were successes?

$$\frac{\text{\# of successes}}{\text{\# of missions}} = \frac{?}{?}$$

Curiosity

The Mars Science Laboratory mission successfully landed the *Curiosity* rover on the surface of Mars in 2012. A rover is a small machine used to explore the surface of a planet.

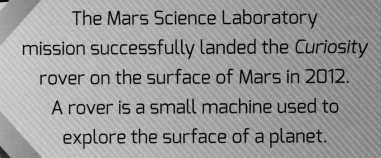

Mariner 6

MISSION LAUNCH DATE	NAME	RESULT
1964	Mariner 3	Failure
1964	Mariner 4	Success
1969	Mariner 6	Success
1969	Mariner 7	Success

ANSWER: According to the chart, 3/4 of the missions were successes.

WHERE'S THE WATER?

People have wondered if life exists or has ever existed on Mars. Life needs water. Scientists thought Mars was completely frozen. However, images in 2015 showed dark streaks on the slopes of craters. This is a sign that water flows during certain seasons on the planet's surface. What will the next mission to Mars discover?

YOUR MISSION

Water may have helped form a group of canyons on Mars called Valles Marineris. It's about 2,500 miles long and 4 miles deep. Earth's Grand Canyon is about 275 miles long and as deep as 1 mile in some places. How much longer and deeper is Valles Marineris?

$$2,500 - 275 = ?$$ $$4 - 1 = ?$$

In 2015, a NASA craft sent back proof that water flows on Mars at times. The search for life continues!

ANSWER: Valles Marineris is about 2,225 miles (3,581 km) longer and 3 miles (5 km) deeper than the Grand Canyon.

21

GLOSSARY

crust: the outermost layer of Earth

data: facts and figures

dense: packed very closely together

gravity: the force that pulls objects toward the center of a planet or star

lava: hot, liquid rock that flows from a volcano

mass: the amount of matter in an object

mission: a task or job a group must perform

orbit: to travel in a circle or oval around something, or the path used to make that trip

solar system: the sun and all the space objects that orbit it, including the planets and their moons

telescope: a tool that makes faraway objects look bigger and closer

tilted: slanted, not straight up and down

volcano: an opening in a planet's surface through which hot, liquid rock sometimes flows

FOR MORE INFORMATION

Books

Capaccio, George. *Mars*. New York, NY: Marshall Cavendish Benchmark, 2010.

Carney, Elizabeth. *Mars*. Washington, DC: National Geographic, 2014.

Sparrow, Giles. *Destination Mars*. New York, NY: PowerKids Press, 2010.

Websites

Mars Exploration
mars.nasa.gov
See pictures, watch videos, track Mars rovers, and ask questions at this website.

Popular Science: Exploring Mars
www.popsci.com/tags/mars
Read a number of articles written about Mars.

INDEX